Introduction

We have come to know and to believe in the love God has for us. God is love, and whoever remains in love remains in God and God in him. — 1 John 4:16

Go and make disciples! The Gospel commissioning recorded in Matthew 28:19 summarizes what evangelization is about: it is about making disciples. In her book *Forming Intentional Disciples,* Sherry Weddell offers us a great opportunity for reflection from two perspectives. First, perhaps the most obvious, is that the disciples whom we are commissioned to "make" ought to be intentional and deliberate about their discipleship. Second, maybe more subtle, is that it offers us a chance to reflect on our own discipleship. Sherry invites us to ponder the current realities of the Catholic Church in the United States, and in so doing she offers us an entry point to ponder our own journey of faith.

This short study guide is presented as a resource that may be used with adult formation groups. The most important thing to remember as we embark on this intentional journey is to share the good news about God's love for us and his desire for an intimate relationship with us.

Ximena DeBroeck, M.A.
Coordinator of Adult and Sacramental Formation
Department of Evangelization, Archdiocese of Baltimore

Acknowledgements

This guide was created in collaboration with my co-workers in the Division of Catechetical and Pastoral Formation at the Archdiocese of Baltimore, to whom I would like to express my gratitude for their contributions:

Dr. Lauri Przybysz, D.Min., Coordinator of Marriage and Family Life

Ruth A. Puls, Director Division of Catechetical and Pastoral Formation

Sr. Sally Russell, SSJ, Coordinator of Curriculum & Catechist Formation

Julie St. Croix, Coordinator of Pastoral Leadership Formation

Chapter 1

GOD HAS NO GRANDCHILDREN

In this chapter, Sherry discusses the alarming statistics that describe the reality faced by the Catholic Church today. What reality is she addressing? A growing number of adults who identify as Catholic do not even understand who Jesus is, let alone what it means to follow him as his disciple. On page 52, she states:

> *We live in a time of immense challenge and surprising opportunity. Millions of Western adults are seeking meaning and hope, and are at least potentially open to the Catholic Faith. At the same time, huge numbers of self-identified Catholics and other Christians are not certain that a personal relationship with God is even possible, or that Jesus is God, or that he is really present in the Eucharist — and their values and decisions reflect it. The majority of Catholics in the West are sacramentalized but not evangelized. They do not know that an explicit, personal attachment to Christ — personal discipleship — is normative Catholicism as taught by the apostles and reiterated time and time again by popes, councils, and saints of the Church.*

NOTES

1. What is your initial reaction to the statistics presented in this chapter?

2. What is meant by "far evangelization," as Sherry describes it beginning on page 35? Can you think of people in your life who need this kind of evangelization?

3. A 2020 poll found that 56% of Catholics who attend Mass weekly or more often don't believe that Jesus is God. How does this impact the results of the 2019 Pew study, which found that only one-third of US Catholics believe in the True Presence of Jesus in the Eucharist?

4. What struck you most in reading the statistics from other Western nations (outside of the United States)? Where do you see the United States following the same trends?

Chapter 2

WE DON'T KNOW WHAT NORMAL IS

1. On page 60, three spiritual journeys are described. What are they? Do you see them as separate or interrelated journeys?

2. In your journey of faith, have you been formed from the perspective of these being separate or interrelated journeys?

3. Reflect on the "normal" values listed on pages 66–67. Which of these values are you most comfortable with, and which one do you think is most challenging to you?

4. What is your own experience of small intentional gatherings of disciples?

5. Are you familiar with the word *kerygma* (see page 66)? What is it?

6. What are your memories of hearing the *kerygma* and your understanding of the *kerygma*? Why do you think the *kerygma* is essential to the journey of faith of a disciple?

In this chapter, Sherry presents excerpts from the document that guided the topics of conversation during the recent gathering of bishops in 2012 to discuss the New Evangelization (the Synod on the New Evangelization). Highlighted multiple times during the synod was the importance of having a relationship with Christ and, thus, with the Father and the Holy Spirit. She states that this relationship involves three spiritual journeys. The manner in which these journeys are nurtured and lived has an impact on our discipleship.

The concept of what is considered "normal" is also presented. Sherry describes that what is perceived as "normal" is skewed. For instance, we have lost the sense that desiring and having a personal relation with Jesus is "normal."

NOTES

Chapter 3

THE FRUIT OF DISCIPLESHIP

Discipleship is NORMAL. Sherry presents the importance of discipleship in the life of the parish: "No matter how many institutions we sustain or how much activity goes on in our parish or diocese, if new intentional disciples are not regularly emerging in our midst, our ministry is not bearing its most essential fruit" (page 94).

This point also applies to each of our lives. No matter how many parish activities we are involved in, if we are not intentional disciples, we will not bear much fruit.

NOTES

1. Reflect on your faith journey. Do you think you are an intentional disciple? What is helping you to, or preventing you from, true discipleship?

2. Ecclesial vocations are mentioned on page 78. The term "ecclesial vocation" in the most basic form indicates a calling lived in the Church, through the Church, and for the Church. Which vocations would you think constitute "ecclesial vocations"?

3. Do you think that marriage and the single life are considered "ecclesial vocations"? Why or why not?

4. Why is discipleship important when discerning any vocation?

5. Reflect on the following passage:

   > *Since we have gifts that differ according to the grace given to us, let us exercise them: if prophecy, in proportion to the faith; if ministry, in ministering; if one is a teacher, in teaching; if one exhorts, in exhortation; if one contributes, in generosity; if one is over others, with diligence; if one does acts of mercy, with cheerfulness.* (Romans 12:6–8)

   What is your understanding of "charisms"? Have you been guided on a path of charism discernment?

6. How are the charisms of your parish community nurtured and brought forward?

Chapter 4

GRACE AND THE GREAT QUEST

1. How do you understand the concept of "grace" in the sacraments?

2. Reflect on the following passage:

   Jesus said to them, "A prophet is not without honor except in his native place and among his own kin and in his own house." So he was not able to perform any mighty deed there, apart from curing a few sick people by laying his hands on them. He was amazed at their lack of faith. (Mark 6:4–6)

   Why do you think "he [Jesus] was not able to perform any mighty deed" in Nazareth?

3. How do you understand the expression "the sacrament will take care of it"? What do you think is missing from that expression?

4. How do you understand the difference between the "validity" and "fruitfulness" of a sacrament?

5. Reflect on the last time that you received formation about the sacraments. What do you remember most about this experience? Has your understanding changed after reading this chapter?

6. Do you think all the formation about sacraments happens exclusively before the sacraments are received? Why or why not?

Sherry brings the reader's attention to two concepts that have been prevalent in our Catholic culture: "the sacrament will take care of it," and "the Church will provide." The reader is then invited to ponder the sacramental life in a new way.

This chapter calls us to reflect on the disposition of the person receiving the sacrament. On pages 107–108, Sherry states:

> Passively receiving a sacrament is not enough. The grace we receive is directly related to the personal faith, spiritual expectancy, and hunger with which we approach the sacrament. St. Thomas [Aquinas] describes how adults who have been validly baptized can receive different effects of grace — or even none at all.

NOTES

Chapter 5

THRESHOLDS OF CONVERSION: CAN I TRUST YOU?

In 1979, Pope John Paul II wrote the apostolic exhortation *Catechesis in Our Time (Catechesi Tradendae)*, which summarized the recommendations made by the Synod of Bishops following their meeting in 1977, when they gathered to discuss the topic of catechesis. The pope then states:

> Nevertheless, the specific aim of catechesis is to develop, with God's help, an as yet initial faith, *and to advance in fullness* and to nourish day by day the Christian life of the faithful, young and old. … To put it more precisely: within the whole process of evangelization, *the aim of catechesis is to be the teaching and maturation stage.* (20) [emphasis added]

It is important to remember that although the aim of catechesis is to bring one's faith to maturity, *this is not a single-step process.* Sherry describes five thresholds or stages that occur in the process of conversion toward intentional discipleship and mature faith. In this chapter, the initial threshold — which is trust — is discussed.

NOTES

1. What are the five thresholds of conversion presented in this chapter?

2. Are these thresholds focused on knowledge of the faith? Is it possible to have a "high" knowledge of the faith and not have experienced conversion?

3. What is the role of trust in the process of conversion and evangelization? What exactly is understood by the term "trust"?

4. Reflect on a close relationship. How did you become close friends? How was trust established? What happened if trust was betrayed?

5. Reflect on your faith journey. Has there been someone who was a "bridge of trust" for you? Have you been a "bridge of trust" for someone?

6. What connection do you see between trust and the countless numbers of Catholics who no longer practice the faith? Discuss your answer.

Chapter 6

THE SECOND THRESHOLD: CURIOSITY

1. After reading this chapter, do you understand curiosity as active or passive? In other words, is it active seeking or casual curiosity?

2. What is the relation between trust and curiosity?

3. Let us reflect again on the passage from John's Gospel:

   > *The next day John was there again with two of his disciples, and as he watched Jesus walk by, he said, "Behold, the Lamb of God." The two disciples heard what he said and followed Jesus. Jesus turned and saw them following him and said to them, "What are you looking for?" They said to him, "Rabbi" (which translated means Teacher), "where are you staying?" He said to them, "Come, and you will see." So they went and saw where he was staying, and they stayed with him that day.* (John 1:35–39)

   Jesus invited his would-be disciples to "come and see." In your own faith journey, have you been invited to "come and see," or have you received information about the faith?

4. Are you likely to invite others to "come and see," or are you more comfortable teaching about all the dogmas of the faith?

5. Reflect on the difference between Jesus as a "topic" of faith formation and Jesus as the personal God who is capable of forming a personal relationship with each individual.

6. Do you think the three basic stages of curiosity (page 149) offer a helpful tool for those involved in faith formation in a parish community?

Once the bridge of trust has been established, Sherry explains, the role of the evangelizer is to help transition to the next threshold, that of curiosity about Jesus Christ. During this threshold people are open to exploring the possibility of a personal relationship with God.

"*Those who don't believe in a personal God and the possibility of a relationship with that God will never be able to move beyond the threshold of curiosity*" (pages 148–149). During this time, it is important to allow people to express their curiosity. This is not the threshold at which we teach all the dogmas of the Church; rather, this is the time when we invite people to reflect on the question, "Who do you think that Jesus is?"

NOTES

Chapter 7

THE THIRD THRESHOLD: OPENNESS

Just as trust is needed in order to move to curiosity, curiosity is needed in order to move to openness. Sherry tells us, "But moving into that threshold is one of the most difficult journeys for twenty-first-century people to make because it demands that we declare ourselves open to the possibility of personal and spiritual change" (page 161).

Moving into this threshold is not the same for everyone. For some, it might only take a weekend experience of attending a truly evangelizing retreat, but for others it might be months, even years, of "testing the waters." This transition occurs without much struggle for only a few people; the majority of people struggle with truly being open to change. Those accompanying someone through this stage need to be very patient. Unfortunately, when we are eager to share the Good News, we fail to exercise as much patience as we should. Many times, an initial openness to change is confused by the evangelizer with intentional discipleship — this can create a greater struggle in the transition toward openness.

NOTES

1. Why is the transition between curiosity and openness a difficult process?
2. What are likely triggers that pave the way to the door of openness? Why do you think the "trigger" opens the way to move to the threshold of openness?
3. How does your parish foster openness with those who inquire about the faith?
4. What are some ways in which you (or your parish) could encourage openness in those who have left the Catholic Church or who are considering leaving because their spiritual hunger is not met?
5. Reflect on times in your own faith journey when you have experienced openness. What was the "trigger"? What was the most valuable experience that helped foster openness for you?
6. What are some ways in which you have fostered openness? What was most challenging?

Chapter 8

THRESHOLDS OF CONVERSION: SEEKING AND DISCIPLESHIP

1. What is the main difference that sets apart the threshold of seeking from the previous three thresholds?

2. What is the primary task of the evangelizer (and the catechist) when someone has reached the threshold of seeking?

3. What connection do you see between seeking and becoming an intentional disciple?

4. How would you companion someone in the seeking stage?

5. Why do you think it is important to address personal sin with seekers? How would you address this topic? Reflect on your own faith journey. How do you understand personal sin?

6. Often the journey toward intentional discipleship is not clearly presented. In fact, there are many pastoral leaders who are not yet disciples. Does this affect your faith journey? How would you treat a leader who is not yet a disciple?

The last two thresholds are a bit different from the other three. They are sometimes called "The Zone." Sherry explains:

> We have found it useful to think of the two thresholds of seeking and intentional discipleship as a whole. … What both thresholds have in common is that they are *active* rather than essentially passive like the earlier thresholds of trust, curiosity, and openness. (page 178)

In order to enter into the threshold of "seeking," there has to be a certainty that a personal relation with God IS possible. Those who seek are looking for the person of Jesus Christ but are not intentional disciples yet. They are seriously thinking about following Jesus. During this threshold the evangelizer continues to model what it means to be a disciple and continues to proclaim the *kerygma.* This is also the threshold best suited for catechesis.

NOTES

Chapter 9

BREAK THE SILENCE

We cannot begin to find solutions to a problem unless we realize there is a problem. Once that happens, we need to name the problem. It is important that we face our current realities. It has been estimated that only 5 percent of parishioners at any given parish are intentional disciples. Prayerfully, we can set goals and a plan of action to help form more intentional disciples.

Sherry offers us much encouragement:

> While *we* cannot make anyone "drop their nets" any more than a gardener can make a seed germinate, we can intentionally and intelligently work to create an environment that is conducive to the growth of personal faith and discipleship. (page 194)

NOTES

1. What specific problem facing our parishes, dioceses, and our Church in general is Sherry discussing in this chapter? Why is this problematic?

2. Most of our formation programs are "silent" about an essential component of the journey of faith. What is that component?

3. What is your understanding of the goals of a "threshold conversation"?

4. Reflect on your faith journey. Did someone ever have a "threshold conversation" with you?

5. How does your understanding of "threshold conversation" change the way in which you would "break the silence"?

6. What aspects of threshold conversations seem most challenging to you? What aspects seem most natural?

Chapter 10

DO TELL: THE GREAT STORY OF JESUS

1. What is the real purpose of evangelization?

2. What do you understand by the statement, "What truly awakens Christian faith 'is not primarily *about* the Church herself'"?

3. Reflect on your faith journey. What story did you hear first?

4. If we could honestly reflect on our faith formation programs, what do you think is most central to them — the teachings of the Church, or the story of Jesus?

5. What does telling the "Great Story" mean for you? What does it mean for our pastoral practices?

6. What elements of the "Great Story of Jesus in Nine Acts" are helpful to your faith journey? Does the story need to be told in this order?

It is important that we accept the sad reality that most people have NOT heard the great story of Jesus. Therefore, as evangelizers we must make a commitment to tell this story. In our zeal to share our own journey, we need to remain mindful to keep things in perspective and to remember that the story of Jesus is most important. Sherry reminds us, "Our own personal witness can help illuminate and make living, compelling, and believable aspects of Jesus's story, *but it cannot take the place of Jesus' story*" (page 210).

The story needs to be tailored to our audiences. The story is unchangeable, but what does change is what parts are shared, when, and in what order. What truly awakens Christian faith "is not primarily *about* the Church herself," but primarily about Christ (see page 215). Sherry offers us a plan of telling the story in a series of nine acts.

NOTES

Chapter 11

PERSONALLY ENCOUNTERING JESUS IN HIS CHURCH

Once the silence is broken, and the story is told, the next evangelization step in forming intentional disciples is to "*create multiple, overlapping opportunities for people to personally encounter Jesus in the midst of his Church*" (page 227).

We need to begin with what we already have in place. Our parishes and our dioceses already have many structures in place. There are many faith formation opportunities for children and for sacramental preparation already available. There is, of course, the golden opportunity of the homily at every Mass. These two opportunities should be revisited, and in Christian charity we should change what needs to be changed so that the story can be heard. Then, we need to consider what could be added to the offerings that we already have available. This is not the work of one or two people alone. This is the apostolate of the entire parish, according to the *charisms* given to all.

NOTES

1. What is your understanding of "charism"? When did you first hear about charisms?
2. Which charisms do you think you have received?
3. How can you help others discover their gifts?
4. Do you think there are any charisms that are not welcomed in many parishes? Why do you think that might be the case?
5. What are some of the structures already in place in your parish that could provide evangelizing opportunities? What would need to be changed in order for these structures to be truly evangelizing?
6. Reflect on your faith journey. Which opportunities have you found (at your current parish or a parish from the past) that have helped you encounter Jesus in his Church?

Chapter 12

MAKING DISCIPLES AND FORMING APOSTLES IN THE NEW MISSIONDOM

1. On page 230, Sherry writes, "*Missiology is the subset of practical theology that focuses on the first proclamation of Jesus Christ and the establishment of his Church where it is not known.* The whole parochial life of the Western Church is going to have to be reevaluated and reshaped around this new understanding of our reality." Why is this the case?

2. What are some of the resemblances that Western Christianity today bears to the early Church?

3. What is a "missiondom conversation"? How can we prepare ourselves to have these conversations?

4. Starting on page 250, Sherry describes three stages of adult Christian development. What are those three stages? What is Sherry's rough estimate of the number of Catholics who have reached the apostolic level of spiritual development? What can we do to change that number?

5. What is the "crucial missing dimension" for spiritual renewal that Sherry discusses in this chapter (beginning on page 269)? What are some ways in which each of us can take responsibility for this essential activity?

As we navigate the new mission territory of the Western world, we need community more than ever before. Spiritual isolation is dangerous, and we must be careful not to make disciples and then abandon them. "Most new disciples need an 'Ananias,' a disciple-companion, or an Ananias-like group of spiritual companions who understand what he or she is experiencing and will walk alongside" (page 262). How has spiritual isolation impacted you personally? How have you seen it affect others? What steps can we take to support the formation of communities of intentional disciples?

NOTES

How can we transmit a living, personal Catholic faith to future generations? By coming to know Jesus Christ, and following him as his disciples.

As we emerge from a pandemic into a post-Christian world, these are times of immense challenge and enormous opportunity for the Catholic Church in the United States. Ten years after it was first published, ***Forming Intentional Disciples*** by Sherry Weddell is still helping scores of Church leaders, parish staff, and all Catholics transform parish life from within. Her book leads you through the steps that will help Catholics enter more deeply into a relationship with God and the river of apostolic creativity, charisms, and vocation that flow from that relationship for the sake of the Church and the world.

This companion study guide will help you transform your parish or small faith community. Created by people who have experienced the transformative impact of discipleship firsthand, this revised edition of the ***Forming Intentional Disciples Study Guide*** provides tools and resources to initiate conversations, share the story of faith, and begin walking the path of discipleship together.

OSV

Inventory No. T2800
ISBN-13: 978-1-63966-055-1
9 781639 660551